# OCEAN
## OF
# EMOTION

AN EXTRACT FROM
THE KEYS OF TRANSFORMATION

# DAVID ASHWORTH

First published by
David Ashworth,
P.O. Box 312, Whitefield, Manchester M45 8PW
www.davidashworth.com
Email: dave@davidashworth.com


© David Ashworth 2008
First Published May 2008


ISBN 978-0-9559067-0-1

Designed and typeset by Chris Peach, www.centricalsolutions.com

Printed by Zrinski, in Croatia

## Contents

## Introduction

This booklet is actually a chapter from a larger work to be published later, but Spiritual Guidance has requested that this information should go out now because there is such an acceleration in the speed of Universal Consciousness, as we move towards the year 2012. Time is running out and there are many who are already falling by the wayside and because of the nature of the shifting consciousness, they cannot see it.

The Ocean of Emotion teaches you how your consciousness works, through an understanding of what is easy to access and what is more difficult to access. The Guidance which brings these images to me is most insistent that evolutionary processes are simple, and with a little determination and practice, you can gently and effectively unlock your own consciousness steadily. The key is to 'stimulate' the deeper self to 'let go' of the patterns and issues which lie beyond our awareness and prevent evolution through fear. If you learn to apply the knowledge contained in these pages, then you will truly be able to accelerate your evolution and achieve a potential beyond your imagination.

*Walking the Path of the Spiritual Warrior*
*Is not the new Rock and Roll.*
*It is the only Rock and Roll,*
*It is the ultimate Rock and Roll.*

Blessings

Dave Ashworth
Prestwich, March 2008

# Ocean of Emotion

The human Subtle Energy System, consisting of the Aura and the Chakras, Emotions and Consciousness is like a deep ocean and in order to begin to stimulate the Evolution of Human Consciousness we need to learn how to understand, navigate and penetrate this ocean. The absolute Key to bring about evolution of consciousness is the ability to enter the depths of the heart and the depths of the heart lie in the deepest part of our Ocean of Emotion.

## A Pathway of Permanent Evolution

Why might we want to access the deep, hidden consciousness within the heart?

- ❤ to unlock our spiritual evolution
- ❤ to release and open our hidden gifts, talents and potential
- ❤ to ascend the ladder of insight
- ❤ to unlock our perception of reality
- ❤ to go beyond illusion
- ❤ to allow a continual unfolding and ascension onto a higher path

All of the above is a representation of Ascension into Truth.

## The Shallows and the Deep

Imagine for a moment descending into the sea. As you enter the water, there is light all around. Daylight penetrates the surface of the water and you can see clearly. Visualise for a moment a clear tropical reef with coral and brightly coloured fish. However, as you descend the density of the water filters out the light. Eventually you reach a point where light cannot penetrate any further and you enter the deep, dark ocean. No ordinary natural light can ever enter this place. You will have seen such images of this darkness on television, usually filmed from a mini submarine with its own light source.

### Fig 1 - Ocean of Emotion

**The Shallows**

Light Penetrates
The Shallows

**The Deep**

No Light Penetrates
The Deep

If we divide the ocean into two distinct areas, and call them The Shallows and The Deep, we can relate these same images to our energy system and consciousness. The Shallows represent the area of our being where light enters, such as the Chakra System and Mental and Emotional Bodies located within the Aura. The Deep represents the place where no light touches, which is the very deep consciousness that is hidden in the Core of the Heart.

Within The Shallows, we are consciously aware of what we are processing at many levels of our mental and emotional lives. Even the emotional patterns that we do not wish to experience or think about are in our awareness at some level. Let us say that to the greater degree, The Shallows are processing the energy and consciousness of our thoughts and emotions in the moment - in the now.

In the deeper darker reaches of The Deep, we touch into the primordial aspects of our Selves. Not only those aspects of who we are at this moment in time in the present incarnation, but also many aspects of ourselves from previous incarnations that are still with us, unresolved, within the core of the heart. Some of these aspects may go back as far as the time when mankind first began to walk upon the Earth, gathering experiences and learning how to exist.

# Fig 2 - The Shallows and The Deep

## The Shallows = Energy

- Awareness at some level
- The Chakra System and The Aura
- Mental and Emotional Processing
- Sense and Feeling
- Light penetrates all these layers

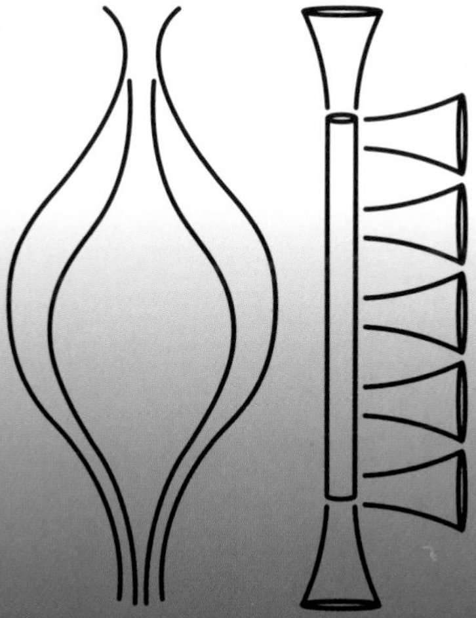

Aura     Chakras

Sub-conscious Barrier = The Cap of The Well of Fears

## The Deep = Consciousness

- Non-awareness of what is within
- The Well of Fears, located within the Steel-like Core of the Heart Chakra
- The deepest point in Human Consciousness
- The Primordial Swamp of the Original Fears which were Created in Earth and which are carried until they are dissolved back into Earth
- The Eternal Memories held within the Fear
- Fear being the Original Darkness
- Density and Mass of Darkness
- No Light penetrates this darkness without power to drive it

> *Jesus said:*
>
> *There is Light at the centre of a man of Light,*
> *and he illumines the whole world.*
> *If he does not shine, there is darkness.*
>
> The Gospel of Thomas

## Whatever is Below, Must Ascend

To unlock the door to the evolutionary pathway, we must find a way of entering the Depths and create movement by bringing Light into the Original Darkness within. We always work from the Deepest point we can access and stimulate movement at that level. As you trigger a response at the deepest level, then whatever is released begins to rise towards the surface.

When movement is created, the darkness within begins to do two things.

- ❤ Firstly, darkness begins to dissolve in the face of Light, and as it dissolves, it loses some of its mass, or weight.

- ❤ Secondly, as it loses weight, it begins to rise from The Deep and enter The Shallows. As it enters The Shallows it enters your awareness and that is when it can begin to affect you.

Original Darkness from The Deep is Fear. These are the fears which have been created through many lifetimes. In certain lifetimes at certain points in time we bring some of that fear back to earth in order to understand it, learn from it and dissolve it. There is a natural process within our deeper consciousness which is governed by your Higher Self and this process releases fear at certain times in your evolutionary development. This often happens at certain ages, such as between the ages of 38 and 42. The greatest external event which causes fear to be released from The Deep and then rise upwards, is when we enter a new aeon such as now, as we enter The Age of Aquarius. As the doors of a new age open, then consciousness speeds up and we begin to attain a new level of perfection. In order to ride this accelerating wave of consciousness we need to lose some of that inner mass of fear and so the natural process of shifting into a new age changes your vibration, which allows fear to leave The Deep.

When fear begins to touch your awareness, as it enters The Shallows, it begins to limit your expression of life. It begins to control you. You find that you have an inability to act or do the things you want to do. You become a prisoner of the fear within you.

We are all prisoners of fear at some level. Even though we are not aware of it, the fears in the darkness of The Deep control us all of the time. However, because we have no awareness of what is contained within The Deep, we don't have any awareness of how those hidden fears control us. The saying below, from The Gospel of Thomas refers to our lack of awareness of what is in The Deep.

*Jesus said:*
*I will give you what no eye has seen,*
*and what no ear has heard,*
*and what no hand has touched*
*and what has not arisen in the heart of man*

The Gospel of Thomas

This saying explains how you cannot see the darkness in the heart without it being illuminated. Jesus says that nobody has awareness of this area of the heart, but He, or his light, will give you (or reveal to you) what is down there. With the present acceleration of the awakening of humanity, certain people, like myself, are now evolved enough to be able to perceive at this level of the heart. The ability to see into The Deep, or The Well of Fears, as it is known, is the key to the evolution of human consciousness.

5

If we did not have this fear or darkness within, we would contain more Light and with more Light, then we would function at a much higher level than we see expressed by humans at their present level of evolution. The whole of humanity at present is based on oppression and control, through the fear of being controlled. It is the 'oppress the other before you are oppressed yourself' mentality. The claim to greatness by all countries who have power is that they obtained that power by crushing other nations. No country claims to be great from benevolence towards others, only by controlling others through fear. But that's another story, and not for these pages.

## The Deep

To commence the process of Evolution of Consciousness, we must go into The Deep, create movement within the darkness within and begin to bring it upwards, through The Shallows, to be exposed and learned from and eventually expelled from our Being and life through dissolving its energy back into the Earth. This is the essence of the saying, 'ashes to ashes, dust to dust.' All fear was originally created in Earth, or in a human life in the Earth plane, and whatever is created in Earth, must return to the Earth. Don't you think you've carried it for long enough?

The first thing to understand about The Deep is that we have virtually no awareness of what is down there. The Core of the Heart is ringed with energy so strong it is like trying to penetrate steel to gain access to the inner cells of the core, known as The Well of Fears (see Fig. 3).

As we plumb the depths of the Core of the Heart, we could say that it is like a primordial swamp of darkness, for many things have been both pushed down there, and fallen down there through many, many lives. One of the Keys to Evolution is the knowledge of how to enter that swamp and begin to both dissolve and raise some of the heaviness of mental and emotional patterns and fears which have sunk to the bottom because of their mass, or weight, not to mention being pushed down there by our sub-conscious mind through denial.

## Fig 3 - The Structure of The Heart Chakra

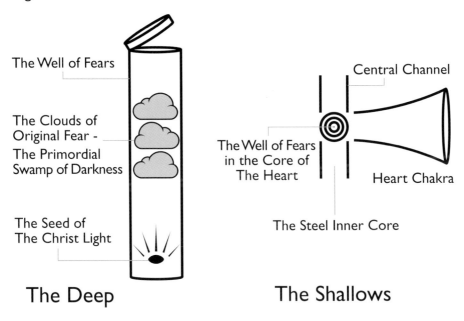

The Well of Fears

The Clouds of
Original Fear -
The Primordial
Swamp of Darkness

The Seed of
The Christ Light

**The Deep**

Central Channel

The Well of Fears
in the Core of
The Heart

Heart Chakra

The Steel Inner Core

**The Shallows**

## Accessing The Deep

The most powerful way we can access all levels of our consciousness, whether The Shallows or The Deep is by penetrating these areas with highly effective energetic tools. It is relatively easy to access The Shallows, using Hypnosis, Neuro-linguistic Programming (NLP), Kinesiology, Emotional Freedom Technique (EFT) and many, many other modalities of energy work and healing, but getting into The Deep is another matter.

- ❤ The Shallows comprise Energy with a touch of Consciousness

- ❤ The Deep is Consciousness, holding onto the dense Energy of Fear

To gain access to The Deep you need power. You need a powerful force which is at the same time subtle and gentle. You need something which can contain both consciousness and intelligence to know what it is doing and power to allow it to do what it knows. Such tools are High Vibrational Evolutionary Essences.

Working with essences on a daily basis will continually push your evolution. For very little effort invested, you can continually unlock the hidden aspects of your Self. What is more, you don't always need to know what you are unlocking. The beauty of working with essences in this way is that they often dissolve the energy within an issue without you having to experience the emotion which might be locked up within that issue. How good is that? So, how do we work to unlock the secrets of The Deep in our Ocean of Emotion?

## Unlocking the Evolution of Your Consciousness

The way to access both levels of the Ocean of Emotion is to use a two-pronged approach which brings light into both distinct areas of The Shallows and The Deep simultaneously. The way we do this is by using different vibrational essences at the same time, to target the individual energies in each specific area. What we need to understand at this point is that whatever we can stimulate to move in The Deep, will rise through The Shallows. So, the key to success is to constantly target and motivate whatever is in The Deep first and then dissolve whatever rises through The Shallows simultaneously.

## Different Vibrations for Different Places

We can break down essences into two distinct areas:

- ♥ Traditional Vibrational Essences
- ♥ High Vibrational Evolutionary Essences

Traditional Vibrational Essences, such as the Bach Flower Remedies, work in the area of The Shallows. High Vibrational Evolutionary Essences work in the area of The Deep.

Human consciousness is accelerating and we are now heading towards a hundred years since Dr. Bach began to harness the vibrations of flowers and show us this amazing hidden and subtle world of consciousness. Those remedies are a reflection of his advanced level of perception at the time. There are those amongst us today who's consciousness is accelerating and opening into the next levels of evolution of consciousness and the essences they create reflect the deeper levels of consciousness that we can now penetrate.

The Essences I have created over the years are a direct reflection of my own amazing transformation. I can now perceive into The Deep in any person, anywhere on the planet. These essences are specifically designed to evolve human consciousness.

## Entering The Deep

The area of The Deep is also known as The Well of Fears.

### Fig 4 - The Well of Fears

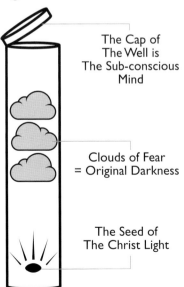

The Cap of
The Well is
The Sub-conscious
Mind

Clouds of Fear
= Original Darkness

The Seed of
The Christ Light

Let us say that The Deep is governed by the sub-conscious mind. The sub-conscious desires to hide the truth within and maintain stillness without change at all times, by denying access to The Deep or The Well. The sub-conscious does not want any waves made, for while everything is in stillness, or locked in fear, it doesn't have to worry about those deeper issues touching your life. If the fears remain in The Well, then they remain outside of your awareness. Why should the sub-conscious mind be concerned this way? Because if the fears from The Deep escape into The Shallows, then your waking consciousness experiences the fear. The sub-conscious will do anything to avoid this.

## Fear of Change

The *modus operandi* of the sub-conscious mind is driven by Fear of Change. The sub-conscious will prevent change at all costs. The Sub-conscious mind rules the domain at the gateway between The Shallows and The Deep.

We could say that the sub-conscious mind is the gateway between these two domains. This gateway, or barrier, is also the Cap at the top of the Well of Fears.

### Fig 5 - The Cap of the Well of Fears

The Shallows

Sub-conscious Barrier

The Deep

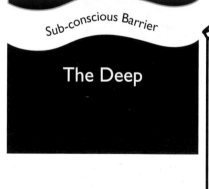

The Barrier between
The Shallows and The Deep
is the Sub-conscious Mind

The Barrier is also
The Cap of The Well of Fears

To achieve evolution, what we must do is deliberately challenge the Fear of Change that is held so sacred by the sub-conscious mind. We want to actively promote a little movement in The Deep or The Well of Fears, in order to bring about evolutionary change in our lives; in order to release active forces that deliberately undermine us. We want to drop an energetic charge into those deep, dark depths and allow it to explode, creating a little movement, momentum and chaos.

## Fig 6 - Creating Movement in The Deep

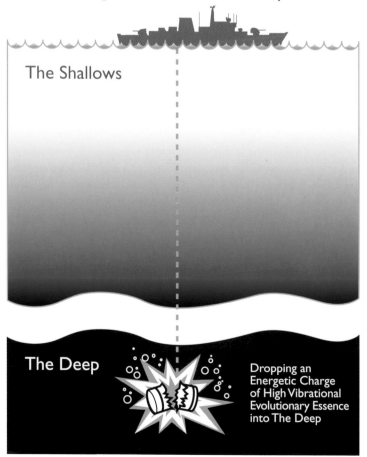

The Shallows

The Deep

Dropping an
Energetic Charge
of High Vibrational
Evolutionary Essence
into The Deep

The subsequent impact of such an explosive device as a High Vibrational Evolutionary Essence will shatter the bonds which hold certain energetic patterns in place. It will begin to break up the mass in the primordial swamp of ancient fears and as the vibrations of the essence create waves and ripples in The Deep, we then attain some movement.

For example, take an issue like Lack of Self-confidence or Unworthiness in a person's life. An issue is always governed by a fear. For example, Lack of Self-confidence might be governed by Fear of Speaking Out. Unworthiness might be governed by Fear of Being Yourself or Fear of Standing in Your Power. The issue might well be expressing itself in this life from situations many lifetimes ago which are now no longer relevant to the learning process, but the energy continues to accompany you into subsequent lives until it is dissolved.

You can't shake the energy off because the bonds that hold it in place are so powerful. Therefore, in order to break these bonds and release this energy, so that it might rise to the surface, you need to apply some subtle force which speaks the same language. That language is vibration, and certain vibrations hold certain conscious patterns in place. If we can discover what the subconscious is holding in place, we can also then discover a vibration that will begin to move it. Therefore, we can target the rigid bonds of the energy pattern which holds tight onto the fear which limits and controls us. As we target the fear with the energy of a vibrational essence, it begins to loosen within the primordial swamp of clouds of fear within The Well. It is then free. It then begins to rise towards The Shallows.

## Releasing the Fears from The Deep

When you can target an issue accurately within yourself, using a high vibrational energy of the optimum penetrative power, then movement occurs. As the anchors which hold the energy pattern deep within the heart dissolve, the energy of the issue begins to rise. Visualise the fears as small clouds of dark energy. Once we have stimulated some movement in The Deep, we need to be prepared to deal with the consequences of that action. We know that once released from captivity in The Deep, the energies are going to rise into the Shallows, therefore we must prepare for their arrival in the mental and emotional areas of our awareness.

As the energy enters your mental and emotional awareness, it begins to restrict you. It begins to hold you prisoner at some level. If you are aware and you can feel it, then this is now a great opportunity to challenge yourself to go beyond the fear. Identify the fear clearly, then understand how it controls you, then challenge yourself to go beyond its power to hold you. However, what most people do automatically is allow the sub-conscious mind to push the fear down again and then nothing becomes resolved.

As you focus and challenge yourself to go beyond what holds you prisoner, that is when courage is released from the heart and the energy of courage begins to help in the process of dissolving the fear energy within The Shallows. This is also where the second prong of our approach comes in.

## Dissolving the Issue in The Shallows

The key to working effectively in The Shallows is to use Traditional Vibrational Essences every single day. By doing this you are targeting and dissolving energy patterns and bringing harmony and balance to your mental and emotional life constantly. Whether you know what you are targeting or not, is not important. What is important is the evolution of your consciousness, and working daily with essences will maximise the clarity of perception within your awareness.

As stronger energies rise from The Deep, they can pass through The Shallows almost unnoticed when being worked upon daily. Practise choosing what you need each day by dowsing or intuition from your choice of Traditional Essences.

## The Flow

The Heart Chakra is the main energetic organ which helps to clear The Shallows. This chakra works like a kitchen extractor fan, constantly sucking at any unwanted energies in the mental and emotional bodies. If there is a lot of unwanted energy in The Shallows, then the heart chakra struggles to keep pace with the heavy work load and in this struggle it will slow down. In turn, this slows down your whole vibration. When the vibration begins to slow down, then you lose your perceptive edge; you sink from Light into Darkness, even though that sinking process is very minute within the grand scheme of things. But, it is the equivalent of a good athlete not training, then when it comes time to run a race, they find themselves coming last. What you must ask yourself is this: Do I want to be as tuned-up as I can be, for very little investment and effort, or do I want to be an 'also ran'? The choice is yours.

As the heart chakra continually vacuums up the debris from within, your whole being is lifted and motivated. What remains un-dissolved at this point is blown out of you through the chakra and returned to the Earth Mother.

## Working with Essences for the Evolution of Consciousness

As you unfold by working with essences daily, your intuition, perception, inner knowing, sensitivity and hidden gifts and talents also unfold. As this happens, then you will begin to understand how such simple tools as essences can open the inner doors to something so mysterious and awe inspiring as the evolution of your consciousness. This is the work I do with people every single day. I help them to unlock that which is within, and the transformation is always tangible and often remarkable. Whether humanity knows it or not, we are all on that journey back to Unity and when the time is right, everyone will begin to awaken and search for the answers they need in order to begin to unlock their own consciousness. One of the most powerful keys you will ever find to the answers you seek are within those tiny, sensitive bottles of consciousness which we call essences.

Try to remember that God didn't make the journey difficult. Why would He? It is ourselves who make the journey difficult and complex, when the truth is always very simple and very obvious, we just try to avoid seeing it.

## Emerging Patterns

As you begin to work with essences on a regular basis, you will discover that certain essences come up for you repeatedly. For example, when choosing the High Vibrational Evolutionary Essences, such as Wheel of Light Essences, Extreme Essences or Sentinel Essences for work in The Deep, you may find that you work with a group of somewhere between 3 to 6 different essences on a regular basis. Also, because things move more slowly in The Deep, you may find that the same essence is required every day for several weeks, or even months. You may find that one or two essences repeatedly come up for periods longer than a year. This is merely showing you that there is something really big that this vibration is working on and the essence is loosening and dissolving it in stages.

When working with the Traditional Essences such as Bach Remedies or Devic Essences, or indeed many other 'flower' or vibrational essences in the area of The Shallows, you will find that a certain core group of essences come up regularly, but you will probably find that you require a different essence from this core group each day. This is because energies move, change and dissolve more quickly in The Shallows.

Reading about the Bach Remedies will help you to understand 'personality types' and you will discover through the essences which regularly come up for you that they reflect your own personality type. As you learn about this it gives you great insight into who you are at a deeper level and what constantly needs to be worked upon.

When you study 'The Readings' associated with the Bach Remedies, rather than concentrating on the Negative Aspects, look at the Positive Aspects. This is telling you more about what the essence is doing for you and where it is taking you, rather than where you are and why. Think positive and move forward. Don't think negative and stay where you are. The Positive Aspects point you in the right direction, telling you what needs to change. When you know what the essence is trying to bring to you, it is then easy to see what lies beneath the surface of The Shallows that is affecting your balance and harmony.

## Summary of The Two Pronged Approach

Use High Vibrational Evolutionary Essences to move and dissolve fears in The Deep, which is located within the core of the heart.

Use Traditional Vibrational Essences such as the Bach Flower Remedies, Devic Essences or similar to dissolve energies in The Shallows.

### To Attain Evolution

Using High Vibrational Essences on a daily basis will provide a Driving Force for Change within and throughout the Consciousness of The Deep.

### To Create a Foundation of Balance and Harmony

Working on a daily basis with the Bach Remedies, the Devic Essences or many other similar Flower and Vibrational Essences will create Harmony and Balance through the subtle bodies of The Shallows.

# Dissolving Fear

All fear rises from The Deep. When fear begins to come up, it is a natural evolutionary process. The fear is the darkness within us; the barrier to true freedom.

## Facing the Fear

The way to deal with fear is to face it head on. This is a process which can be learned. Like everything else that you learn, it takes a little practise. The more you practise 'allowing' fear to touch you, the better you get at 'allowing' it to dissolve or pass through you.

This is what you do. When you feel the fear coming up, you have to stop everything you are doing and look right into the eye of the fear. Allow the fear to wash over you like a wave of water. Don't flinch or move an inch out of its way, if you can help it. Stand four-square and stare right into it. Feel the fear with every ounce of your senses; every aspect of your being. Allow the fear to overwhelm you; to take you.

## This can be a Frightening Process

Make no mistake, feeling the fear can be very frightening. It can even be terrifying as it overwhelms and consumes you, but fear is only energy, it *cannot* hurt you. Sure, it is scary and it can throw your emotions into turmoil, but it *cannot* hurt you. However, it can hold you captive or make you run for the rest of your life if you do not face it.

Sometimes the fears are small and sometimes the fears are huge, but the effect you can have on them is the same. As you learn to stand in the fear and feel it, you will discover that your courage actually dissolves it as it touches you. That's right, *your* courage dissolves the fear.

If the fear is small, as you dissolve it you will never experience it again. It will be gone forever. Not just for this lifetime, but forever. If it is a big fear, a major fear or what can be termed a life fear, it will consist of more energy. In this case, you will find that you dissolve it in stages. As you allow it to do its worst and you stand in its way in defiance, your courage will activate from within your heart and dissolve a huge portion of it each time it comes up. Once it has risen and you have faced it, then it often doesn't reappear again for many months or even years. As you practise facing and dissolving fear, your vibration goes up and you evolve, this means that when those bigger fears reappear again, you will tackle them more easily. Even the biggest fears can be dealt with in a single lifetime using this method.

When the fear dissolves, it is gone forever. It never comes back. You have beaten it. You have allowed it to try to overwhelm you and it has failed. It failed because the love of God which is in the core of your heart is stronger than that impostor of darkness, the fear. Light overcomes darkness, every time. Trust the power of God within your heart to dissolve the fear.

## Stepping beyond Fear and into Light

Each ounce of fear that is dissolved from within The Deep is replaced by Light. Therefore, as you constantly work to understand and dissolve fear, you are continually learning to step into higher Light. As more Light enters your being, you begin to evolve. Sometimes you can go through tremendous shifts in a short period of time, but more commonly, the evolutionary process unfolds in a steady manner, slowly bringing you through different vibrational levels which allow you to touch moments of clarity of revelatory proportions.

These mini revelations enable you to 'feel' and to 'know' at the deepest point of human consciousness that you have shifted from one level to another. When one of these 'realisation' moments touches you, the inner knowing is undeniable and the elation dramatic and intoxicating. Retrospection is often the teacher and when you connect at that level you suddenly see how you have moved and changed. The important thing to then note is that, although life goes on with its daily ups and downs, your base line vibration will have shifted, and when that happens, it can *never* drop back down again.

# Essences to Access The Shallows

The best advice I could ever give you in terms of finding tools for self-transformation is to buy yourself a full set of Bach Remedies. It is a one-off investment and they will last you for years. Working with these on a daily basis is perhaps the most important step you can take for your own Spiritual Evolution. Don't expect changes overnight when working towards evolution, however, miracles do happen. Often it is other people who notice you are changing and then tell you. Often we cannot perceive our own changes initially, but if you keep a journal, as you look back over the weeks and months it is amazing how the 'little things' suddenly illuminate your consciousness as to how much you have really moved.

# Emerald Heart Bach Remedy Kit
## £165 + P&P (saving a huge £128 off individual component price)

David has combined the original signatures of each Bach Flower Remedy, as originated by Dr. Edward Bach, together with the Light of The Emerald Heart to bring you these unique vibrations.

Each complete kit contains the 38 traditional Bach Remedies, plus 1 Anxiety Essence, for emergencies or stress, together with a 10ml bottle of The Emerald Heart essence, and an 'at a glance' leaflet for quick identification of what you need at any given moment in time.

So invest in a full Emerald Heart Bach Remedy Kit
and treat yourself to these high quality spiritual tools
co-created specifically for self-transformation

To order your complete Bach Kit contact: dave@davidashworth.com
or call +44 (0) 161 772 0207

**British Association of Flower Essence Producers (BAFEP):**

The BAFEP website lists many of the essence producers in the United Kingdom. You will find a wealth of Traditional *and* High Vibrational Essences here. Also, if you search the internet for 'Flower Essences' you will find producers all over the world. You can then dowse or intuit who is the best person or the best essences for you to work with.

Tel: 01392 832005                    Web: www.bafep.com

**British Flower and Vibrational Essence Association (BFVEA):**

The BFVEA supports everything to do with essences, training and practitioners. You can apply for membership or subscribe to their magazine, *Essence*.

Web: www.bfvea.com

## General Guidance

Don't be restricted in any way to the essences or information mentioned in my book. Each person's path is an individual journey and you must work with the tools that you are drawn to by your heart. So, if you feel you need to work with one range of essences or another, then follow your heart. If you feel you need to work with one person or another, then follow your heart. That is how you will find your own truth.

# Essences to Access The Deep

This section is about my own ranges of High Vibrational Evolutionary Essences. These reflect my evolutionary journey to where I am at this point on the path. As a direct result of being guided to obtain these essences, then working with them constantly, I have unfolded through many stages where I have been given the most amazing insights into the nature of humanity and the evolution of consciousness. I have been shown where we are in time and space with regard to the awakening and unfolding of humanity through the Age of Aquarius and the speeding up of consciousness as we progress towards the year 2012, as associated with the Mayan Prophecies and Calendar. All my work is based upon my own insights and the guidance which is continually given to me. However, it is also interesting to note how many others are awakening at a similar level around the world, having similar insights into the nature of reality and how it is changing. Indeed, we live in the most incredibly exciting times and when you can learn how to surf the Wave of Time, which we will look at in another book, then truly your life moves and changes by the second at times and the buzz is electric.

During my journey I have been seeded phenomenal and original streams of Light, such as The Wheel of Light and The Emerald Heart, these have enabled my partner, Denise, and I to develop The Emerald Heart School which teaches others how to work at such a high level, where it is possible to see and perceive into the deepest aspects of the human consciousness, to discover what lies within the Well of Fears, within The Deep.

The Wheel of Light

The Emerald Heart

By then targeting those issues in The Deep with appropriate essences, a complete evolutionary event can be brought about within the person's life that leads to true transformation.

## Visionary

I am a visionary; a trailblazer, philosopher; an original thinker and doer; an author. As my own evolution continues to unfold, I continually roll back the boundaries of what we consider possible in spiritual work. In a long career at the top of my field I have constantly moved from one level to the next, year after year, continually transforming and bringing new concepts into the world of healing and spiritual evolution.

However, it all began very simply, with being guided to visit some of our ancient sacred places, such as stone circles, to harness vibrations to make those first essences. At the time, I was a well-established healer, working with crystals and other people's essences, but also very connected with the nature-spirit consciousness, the realms

The Trippet Stones

of the Devas, through my Earth Healing work and Geomancy, and so those first essences were called The Devic Essences.

## The Devic Essences - A Range of 41 Essences

Devil's Arrows, South

Although my own journey had been somewhat rapid and extreme in the way I had unfolded since my original awakening in the late 1980s, the real acceleration into true evolution began with the creation and subsequent use of The Devic Essences. Initially, I considered that I was being guided to create these to help my clients, but as I worked with them, both the essences and I began to evolve. It was as if the consciousness of each was awakening the other.

**Key:** Traditional/High Vibrational Essences which can access both The Shallows and The Deep.

## The Wheel of Light Essences - A Range of 16 Essences

My development was continuing apace when I was suddenly given three new essences by spiritual transmission. This was a new way of delivering them to me and was a sign that things were moving up a level.

It was Easter Monday 2004, the day of Resurrection, and I was given a Trinity of Essences in as many hours. They came out of the blue in one mad rush. The essences were Enlightenment, Awareness and Quickening. Many more essences would follow over the next couple of years to complete The Wheel

of Light Range and I was sent far and wide to collect the energy signatures. The Wheel of Light pushed me much further and faster than ever before.

**Key:** High Vibrational Essences, unlocking The Deep to bring Evolution.

The Great Pyramid, Giza

## The Extreme Essences - A Range of 11 Essences

The first of the Extreme Essences was born in Sweden in August 2005. It was a one-off and when I made it the energy that came through was indeed extreme. However, nothing then happened for a whole year until I was given information for another ten essences in one fell swoop. The rest of the Extremes were all channelled through a tree, and as with all my essences have a fascinating tale to tell, so please have a look on the website to read the full story.

The Rectory Oak

**Key:** High Vibrational Essences to access the oldest hidden emotions of The Deep.

## The Sentinel Essences - A Range of 4 Current Essences

The first of the Sentinels arrived at the beginning of 2006 and they are still unfolding. It may be some time before we have the full set, although I have been told what they are before they arrive. We are currently using four essences in this range and there will be six eventually.

**Key:** High Vibrational Essences to open the hidden inner doorways of consciousness.

## Unlocking the Beauty within You

Each range of essences has been a great teacher in the way they have arrived and they have taken me on a truly magnificent journey into ever expanding consciousness, allowing me to blossom into the being I am today. A person with gifts and talents that I could never have imagined a few years before.

For this past number of years, I have been unlocking this same beauty in others using such Keys of Transformation as Essences and Light. This book is designed to help you discover a pathway to unlocking your own hidden potential with the understanding that if these new High Vibrational Evolutionary Essences can do what they did for me, then they can do it for you, also.

## The Laws of Evolution

You will become Empowered by learning from this book. But, as all learning comes from experience, don't expect it to happen overnight. You must work at it diligently, over a period of time. However, if you get stuck pick up a phone and work with a practitioner, healer or therapist. We learn by doing, and one of the first things that you will learn is that you can't do it all by yourself. Knowing the first two Laws of Evolution will guide you:

## The First Law of Evolution is -

❤ You cannot walk the path alone

## The Second Law of Evolution is -

❤ You must learn to reach out for help

## Experience, Knowledge and Wisdom

❤ It is by Doing that you gain Experience

❤ It is through Experience that you gain Knowledge

❤ It is from Knowledge that you gain Wisdom

## What am I waiting for?

This is the next question you should be asking yourself. As I have worked over the years helping hundreds of people to transform, the one issue that comes up over and over again is that almost nobody reaches out for help until it is far too late. I then have to spend months in bringing them up to speed, before I can begin the process of unlocking their evolution.

Nobody seems to be able to see how fast the universe is accelerating and so many are being left behind by their lack of understanding. If you could touch the speed of the universe, you would be astonished at how fast the shifts are coming, but when your vibration is not at a level where you can perceive the shifts, then it is impossible to understand. One thing is for certain, evolution will not come to those who wait, but begin to Seek and you will surely be Guided to what you need. The key to Spiritual Evolution is to be pro-active.

## Start Now

At the back of the book are lists of my High Vibrational Evolutionary Essences. You can begin to unlock your evolution right now, by dowsing what you need from these lists. Alternatively, look on my essence websites and see what feels good and right to you, or give us a call and have an in depth consultation where The Guides can advise you how to unlock your consciousness.

Also, read about Essence Programs on the website.

There is only one thing that ever stops you attaining true spiritual evolution, and that is your Self. So, what are you waiting for?

## The Emerald Heart

You can also review The Emerald Heart website at www.emerald-heart.co.uk.

In here you will find additional Practitioners to myself, trained in using Evolutionary Essence Programs, and also details of training programs with The Emerald Heart School.

# About the Author

*Come to the edge, he said.*
*They said: We are afraid.*
*Come to the edge, he said.*
*They came.*
*He pushed them. . . and they flew.*

Apollinaire

After a somewhat traumatic spiritual awakening in the late 80s, Dave quickly developed an ability to see subtle energies, particularly those in the Earth and in nature. After a great deal of study and application of his burgeoning gifts and talents, he commenced a career in Geopathic Stress Investigation and Geomancy using Earth Acupuncture techniques. Also developing simultaneously as a healer, he worked and taught many aspects of subtle energy work, eventually running a highly successful practise in Manchester for many years.

Around 1998 and into the turn of this new century, his already unique gifts and abilities began to unfold at an incredible rate. He passed through many inner trials as his original awakened state accelerated into something quite phenomenal. He was given so much by the Universe that even now, he says that it is difficult to believe it happened. However, it was not an easy path and there were great difficulties as the Universe pushed him relentlessly into ever new territory as his consciousness opened to a point where he could see and perceive into the deepest places in human consciousness of anyone, anywhere.

Dave says, "I was given, and taught how to use, The Keys of Transformation that would unlock the evolution of human consciousness in others." A weighty responsibility, but at the same time, it was given in stages as he learned how to dissolve Darkness and then hold and manifest Spiritual Light in ever increasing amounts.

His pathway was guided every step of the way and he was shown how to continually unlock his own consciousness, although in the early days he didn't understand entirely what was happening or why, until hindsight brought the clarity. Some of the tools that were given were the most amazing Vibrational Essences, encoded by spiritual transmission to unlock whatever barriers he had to pass through in order to unfold. He was also gifted with the most penetrating ability to perceive the limitations and blockages to evolution in others. Also, his source of guidance continually gave him detailed visions similar to the illustrations in this book, showing how subtle energy systems and deeper consciousness worked and how to access them to bring evolution to those who were ready to seek it.

His healing practise eventually gave way to spiritual teaching and evolutionary work, as he shared the knowledge of his own transformation, helping others to unlock and unfold their own hidden gifts and talents. The same essences, which were given for his own journey, proved to be a series of the most amazing keys, that when connected with a penetrating stream of Light, would illuminate and bring change to the lives of others. Dave has used these Keys of Transformation to bring evolution to countless people around the world. When asked how he works, this is what he replied.

"We are incredibly unlimited in what we can do and be. The God-consciousness is seeded within us and we are entering the age where it is awakening. Some of us have been awakened quickly, so that we can guide others. We have been taken way beyond healing ability and into evolution and given the understanding of how to access the darkness that enslaves all of humanity. Through my own journey of transformation, I have learned that every barrier to progression that is placed before me, is a learning process that dissolves darkness and brings me into ever higher Light. You become so attuned to when the God-consciousness places a challenge in your path, that you know that there is no choice but to constantly find the courage to pass through that challenge. When you have learned how to do this, then you can teach others and the Universe brings them when they are ready."

*Our deepest fear is not that we are inadequate.*
*Our deepest fear is that we are powerful beyond measure.*
*It is our Light not our Darkness that most frightens us.*

Marianne Williamson

"When they have the courage to come, I bring them to the edge of the fear that limits them, I touch it and open it to them. Then I push them through it with an intensity of Light that is impossible to imagine. It is their own Light, from the God within them. I push them like a mother bird pushes the chicks out of the nest. Then they fly… and it is glorious to behold. And, Marianne Williamson's words above are the truth of it all. It is only the fear of your own Light which keeps you in Darkness."

## Dave's work Today

Dave has been writing since 1999, his guidance constantly giving him new information for spiritual evolution. However, much of this work has been held back from publication until now, as whenever he has tried to publish, guidance has stopped the process, insisting 'they are not ready.' As we enter 2008 there is now an increased acceleration and much of Dave's work will begin to stream forth, beginning with Ocean of Emotion and followed later in the year with The Keys of Transformation, Book One.

When you can Ride the Wave of Time, which is one of the concepts to be published soon, your life and work constantly changes as you bend and flow with Universal direction and guidance from within. At the present time, Dave's work is divided between consultations with clients, teaching the Emerald Heart students, workshops and the ever-present writing. He says: "I am enthusiastic about the speed at which universal consciousness is unfolding, but frustrated at the lack of the ability of others to see what is happening and take appropriate action to keep up with the changes. By the same token, we could say that everything is unfolding exactly as it should, in this game of infinite possibilities, that we call life".

## Choose Your Essences

### DEVIC ESSENCES

**Key:** Traditional/High Vibrational Essences which can access both The Shallows and The Deep

### The English Sacred Sites

01  Beech Hill Stones

02  Boscawen No. 1

03  Boscawen No. 2

04  Boscawen No. 3

05  Devil's Arrows North

06  Devil's Arrows South

07  Druid's Circle

08  Merry Maidens

09  Pipers No.1

10  Pipers No.2

11  Pipers No.3

12  Stripple Stones Henge

13  Swinside

14  Trippet Stones No.1

15  Trippet Stones No.2

16  Trippet Stones No.3

### The Welsh Sacred Sites

17  Carreg Coetan

18  Gorse Fawr

19  Pentre Ifan

20  St. Lythans

21  The Hanging Stone

22  Ysbyty Cynfyn

### The Scottish Sacred Sites

23  Callanish Moon

24  Callanish Sun

25  Clava Cairns

26  Lady Well No. 1

27  Rosslyn Chapel

28  Samye Ling Monastery

## WHEEL of LIGHT ESSENCES

**Key:** High Vibrational Essences, unlocking The Deep to bring Evolution.

# OCEAN of EMOTION

## EXTREME ESSENCES

**Key:** High Vibrational Essences to access the oldest hidden
emotions of The Deep.

### Negative Neutralisers

01  Tibble Labyrinth

02  Extreme Anger

03  Extreme Despair

04  Extreme Fear

05  Extreme Hate

06  Extreme Sorrow

### Positive Enhancers

07  Extreme Courage

08  Extreme Happiness

09  Extreme Hope

10  Extreme Joy

11  Extreme Love

## SENTINEL ESSENCES

**Key:** High Vibrational Essences to open the hidden inner
doorways of consciousness.

01  Completion

02  Connection

03  Unification

04  Creation

# Websites

Each range of essences has its own website with help pages, but all of them can also be accessed through David's website at www.davidashworth.com, then follow the link which says 'Essence Files'.

Devic Essences:            www.devic.co.uk

Wheel of Light Essences:   www.wheel-of-light-essences.co.uk

Extreme Essences:          www.extreme-essences.co.uk

Sentinel Essences:         www.sentinel-essences.co.uk

David Ashworth:            www.davidashworth.com

# How to Take Essences

The usual way to take an essence is by two or three drops under the tongue or in a glass of water, and then drink the water. Another excellent way is to put three drops in a bottle of water and sip from that during the day. When taken orally, putting the tip of the tongue on the roof of the mouth behind the front teeth, links the central and governing meridians together. This can speed up the effect and also take the energy deeper. You can experiment with other methods, too: Try a drop on the crown of the head - I have known this to annul a headache within seconds; try a couple of drops on the pulse point, on the inside of the wrists, then place the insides of the wrists together forming a cross, and hold or rub gently. All the meridians of the body run through the wrists and the information from the essence can be taken into the system very quickly via this route.

# When to Take Essences

It is best to take essences between meal times, when the physical body is not busy using energy to process digestion. As a rule of thumb, I advocate first thing in the morning and last thing at night, with another slot somewhere in the middle of the day.

## Contact Us

### www.davidashworth.com

Dave's website contains a mass of information about his Spiritual Evolution work. Working one-to-one via telephone consultation, Dave can see into your deepest consciousness, then using the advanced spiritual process of Essence Programs, we can help you bring about true transformation of your consciousness. See Essence Programs in the website for more details.

### Contact us:

- ❤ General Enquiries
- ❤ Help with Choosing Essences
- ❤ Consultations for Guidance and Evolution
- ❤ Revealing Truth Workshops for Spiritual Evolution
  (If you would like to host a workshop, please get in touch)

### Telephone: +44 (0)161 772 0207

Email: dave@davidashworth.com or denisemcavoy1@aol.com

### Learning to Dowse

Denise McAvoy runs a series of one-day workshops in pendulum dowsing, essences and nutrition. You can review these at: www.denisemcavoy.com

### Essence Information

There is a wealth of information on each of the essences in their respective websites and these can be accessed through my home page at: www.davidashworth.com, then click Essence Files in the navigation at the top of the page.

# The Keys of Transformation,

*Book 1, Birth of a New Light*

This new work by David Ashworth takes you on a journey through time from the beginning of the 19th century and demonstrates how the gates of the Age of Aquarius have begun to open. It 'keys' you in to the time-line so that you become a part of it, helping you to understand who you are and why you are here at this time.

Introducing new concepts to explain what is happening as we speed towards the year 2012,

the book shows how many who think they are up-to-speed are actually being left behind through their lack of understanding of what is happening as Universal Consciousness accelerates dramatically. There comes a point where you can't perceive the change any longer because it goes beyond understanding. It goes beyond mind. This is when people become lost and continue with the illusion that everything is okay and on course.

This book guides you in the ways of awakening to a point where you cannot only see and perceive what is happening, but become a part of it.

*To be published in Autumn 2008.*

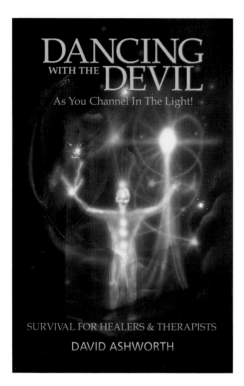

# Dancing with The Devil as You Channel In The Light

David Ashworth's highly successful book, Dancing with the Devil as you Channel in The Light was originally published in 2001 and is now in its fourth printing.

In the ever-expanding world of healing and spiritual awakening, this original work has become an essential part of the Lightworker's library, helping to open the vision, perception and consciousness of all who read it. A book for novices and experienced healers alike, it explodes many myths and misconceptions, helping healers to truly step into their own power through sharing a greater understanding of the fundamentals of the invisible world around us.

Signed copies from the author can be obtained at:
www.davidashworth.com    £14.99 inc. p&p